200 Words

your child will read
by the end of
Grade 2

by Liz Ludewig

BARRON'S

All inquiries should be addressed to:
Barron's Educational Series, Inc.
250 Wireless Boulevard
Hauppauge, New York 11788
http: //www.barronseduc.com

ISBN-13: 978-0-7641-7915-0
ISBN-10: 0-7641-7915-2

Printed in China

9 8 7 6 5 4 3 2 1

Table of Contents

Introduction.............................. 3

Word Groups 4

Decoding Tips 5

Word Group 1 Activities 9

Word Group 2 Activities 19

Word Group 3 Activities 29

Word Group 4 Activities.......... 39

Word Group 5 Activities.......... 49

Word Group 6 Activities 59

Word Group 7 Activities 69

Word Group 8 Activities 79

Word Group 9 Activities 89

Word Group 10 Activities 99

Mixed Word Group
Activities 109

Answer Keys 130

Welcome to 2nd grade!

*What an exciting year for you and your child. Learning to read is a wonderful experience, one that will open your child to a world of possibilities. This book is written for the developing reader. It is designed to enrich the learning that is happening in your child's school. Your child has learned many words that can be read using phonics skills. The words in this book are frequently used sight words, words that are not easily decoded and are often learned in context. **200 Words Your Child Will Read by the End of Grade 2** encourages learning through the use of fun activities that give your child an opportunity to read, write, and use the words in context.*

The sight words in this book are divided into ten groups of twenty words each. Your child will have fun moving from activity to activity as their reading confidence grows. As your child works through the pages of this book you can join in by helping to make sure he or she knows what to do. Read the directions with your child and show them how to use the pictures or illustrations as clues to read the words.

Another outstanding feature of this book is the accompanying CD-ROM of reading activities. This CD provides more activities using each word group. The words are seen in the context of a story and are reinforced through a series of fun activities that include word finds, fill-in-the-blank, and story sequencing.

Enjoy this book with your child. Enjoy helping your child become a better reader. Enjoy this special time with your child, for soon he or she will be in 3rd grade.

Word Groups

Word Group 1

after	Monday	tomorrow
before	or	try
busy	Saturday	Tuesday
every	saw	Wednesday
Friday	Sunday	work
happy	Thursday	yesterday
leave	today	

Word Group 2

cold	I'm	summer
don't	isn't	warm
fall	it's	when
flower	I've	winter
grow	sky	won't
hasn't	snow	you're
I'll	spring	

Word Group 3

all	friend	sleep
boy	girl	those
brother	laugh	took
care	mother	watch
children	must	whole
family	our	woman
father	people	

Word Group 4

about	house	school
blue	large	second
build	long	third
draw	look	where
first	orange	who
green	picture	yellow
here	pretty	

Word Group 5

across	knew	through
become	know	two
belong	night	very
does	one	water
everyone	should	why
great	something	your
jump	this	

Word Group 6

again	heard	right
animal	how	show
because	left	special
both	little	until
brought	loud	use
could	quiet	what
found	ready	

Word Group 7

almost	follow	too
around	foot	tooth
been	have	were
buy	head	which
carry	other	would
close	shout	you
down	since	for

Word Group 8

always	from	soft
answer	goes	some
are	just	start
between	once	story
book	put	upon
finish	read	write
really		

Word Group 9

another	only	teeth
any	out	thank
ask	over	their
by	please	think
guess	said	thought
now	soon	wear
off	sorry	

Word Group 10

either	new	there
enough	next	these
many	none	they
more	paper	toward
much	piece	walk
need	sing	was
never	talk	

How many letters are in the alphabet? The alphabet is made up of twenty-six letters.
a b c d e f g h i j k l m n o p q r s t u v w x y z

The alphabet can be divided into two groups.
Vowels (a, e, i, o, u) and sometimes y
Consonants (b, c, d, f, g, h, j, k, l, m, n, p, q, r, s, t, v, w, x, y, z)

(Y) can be a vowel only when it is in the middle or at the end of a word.
y = i (example — my)
y = e (example — baby)
ay = a (example — play)

Why does the (y) in my sound like (i), like (e) in baby, and like (a) in play?
(y) will sound like (i) when it is at the end
    of a word that has no other vowels.
(y) will sound like (e) when it is at the end
    of a word that has another vowel or vowels in it.
(y) will help make the (long a sound) when
    it is with the letter (a).

How are vowels different from consonants?
Vowels make at least two sounds (long and short).
Consonants usually make just one sound; exceptions are (c), (g), and (x).
c = c like in cat
c = c like in circle
g = g like in go
g = g like in giraffe
x = x like in x-ray
x = ks like in six

Vowels make at least two sounds, so how do you know which sound to use?
The key is to look at the number of vowels.

Short-Vowel Rule: when a word has only one vowel, it is usually short.
Examples are <u>hop</u>, <u>mad</u>, <u>pet</u>, <u>hid</u>, and <u>gum</u>.

Long-Vowel Rule: When there are two or more vowels in a one-part word or
syllable, the vowel is usually long; for example, <u>road</u>, <u>please</u>, <u>gave</u>, and <u>like</u>.

Let's take a closer look. Look at the word <u>road</u>. It has two vowels. The first vowel in the word is (o). The first vowel is the vowel that determines the sound. When a word has two vowels, the sound will be the first letter's name. The second vowel doesn't make any sound, but it has a really important job, because even though it makes no sound, it is a sign for your brain to say the long sound for the first vowel.

When you are figuring out a word, look at the vowels. Think if there is one vowel or more than one. If there is only one vowel, use the short sound for the vowel in the word. If there are two or more vowels, say the long vowel sound for the first vowel.

Here are some examples.

mad — You see one vowel; therefore the (a) is short.

made — You see two vowels; therefore the (a) is long. The letter (e) was a sign for your brain to say the (long a) sound.

However, when there is only one vowel in a word and it comes at the end of the word, it is usually long. Examples are <u>go</u>, <u>me</u>, <u>so</u>, and <u>we</u>.
Note: The long- and short-vowel rules are general guidelines; some words do not follow these basic rules.
The short-vowel rule says that when there is only one vowel, the word should have a short sound, so why doesn't car have the (short a) sound?

It is because it is an r-controlled vowel word.

Usually, if a vowel is followed by an (r) and there is no other vowel in the word, the (r) will control the vowel and make it take on a whole new sound.

R-controlled vowels do not allow the vowel to say its long or short sound.
Examples: <u>park</u>, <u>her</u>, <u>girl</u>, <u>hurt</u>, <u>fort</u>

When (ar) is together, the (ar) makes the sound (r). The letters (er), (ir), and (ur) all say the same sound, but spell it differently. Sometimes (or) can also say the same sound that (er), (ir), and (ur) say. However, the main sound for (or) is or like in fork.

Memory aid for er, ir, ur, and sometimes the (or) sound.
Think of a rooster on a fence. He can wake up the animals in the barnyard by crowing er, ur, ir, or even or. (Note: They all sound about the same, but are spelled differently.)

Tips for Decoding Words with More than One Word Part or Syllable

Big words don't have to be difficult:

Bigger words must be broken into smaller parts to be decoded, for example, <u>kitten</u>.

If a word has double consonants, divide between the double consonants, like in <u>kit/ten</u>.

If a word has two consonants side by side, for example, <u>admit</u> (<u>ad/mit</u>), divide between the consonants and follow basic long- and short-vowel rules. Other examples are <u>kid/ney</u>, <u>ex/plain</u>, <u>con/crete</u>, and <u>ad/vice</u>.

Note: Blends are generally not divided, for example, <u>scat/ter</u>. Do not break up the (sc) blend. Divide between the two (t's) and use the r-controlled sound.

Vowels and Their Sounds
Long/Short and Controlled by (r)

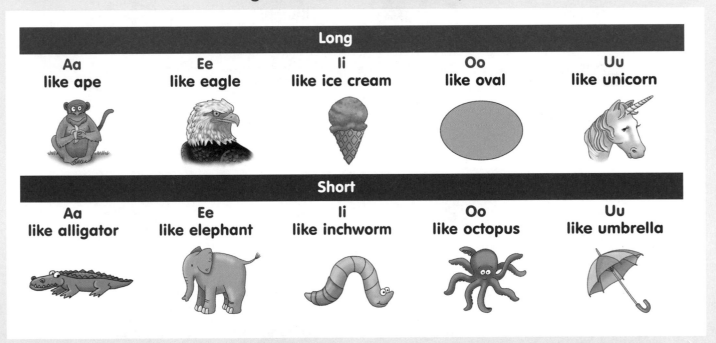

Long				
Aa like ape	Ee like eagle	Ii like ice cream	Oo like oval	Uu like unicorn

Short				
Aa like alligator	Ee like elephant	Ii like inchworm	Oo like octopus	Uu like umbrella

Note: The vowel (Aa) makes three sounds: (long Aa), (short Aa), and the (uh) sound as in (short u). Examples include the following: away, ago, affectionate, ahead, about, agree, afraid, among, around, awake, and awhile.

R – controlled	ar = r like in car	er = er like in fern	ir = ir like in bird
or = or like in fork	ur = ur like in purse	ar = or like in collar	or = er like in color

Note: (er), (ir), (ur), and occasionally (or) are pronounced the same, but spelled differently.   7

More Decoding Tips

You know the sound (t) makes and you know the sound (h) makes. Why then does (th) make a sound that doesn't sound like either letter sound?

It is because when (h) is paired with some consonants, something unusual happens. The consonants take on new sounds that don't sound like the letters normally do.

Special Sounds with (h)

sh
as in
sheep

wh
as in
whale

gh
as in
ghost

gh
as in
laugh

th
as in
thumb

gh
as in
night

ch
as in
chair

ph
as in
elephant

Blends
Blends aren't tricky because the letters sound like they should. What are blends?
Blends are two consonants that are sounded together, but you can hear each letter in the pair.

The most common are the (l), (r), and (s) blends. Blends are found in the beginning, middle, and end of words.

A list of blends follows: br, cr, dr, fr, gr, pr, tr, bl, cl, fl, gl, pl, sc, scr, sk, sl, sm, sn, sp, spl, spr, sq, str, and sw. (tw is another, less common blend.)

ABC Train

Put the words on each car of the train in ABC order.
Start at the engine and end at the caboose.

1. _____   2. _____   3. _____   4. _____

5. _____   6. _____   7. _____   8. _____

Word Group 1 9

Be a Word Detective!

Find each of these words hidden in the word search below. Words can be vertical, horizontal, backwards, or diagonal.

Word Box

tomorrow	leave	Friday	today
work	before	Monday	try

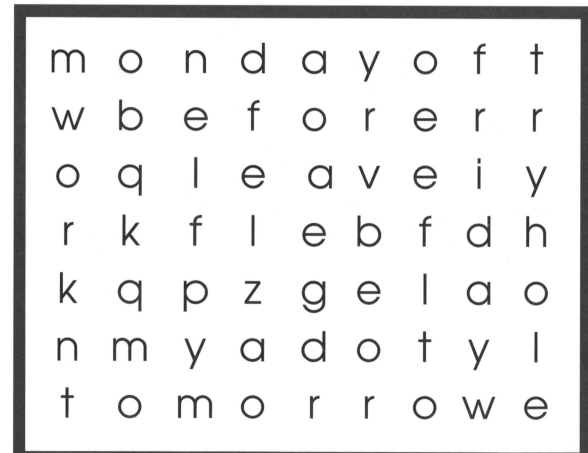

```
m o n d a y o f t
w b e f o r e r r
o q l e a v e i y
r k f l e b f d h
k q p z g e l a o
n m y a d o t y l
t o m o r r o w e
```

All About Me

Draw a picture of yourself.
Then write <u>yes</u> or <u>no</u> after each sentence.

1. **I go to school on Monday.** _____

2. **I brush my teeth before I go to bed.** _____

3. **I ate ice cream yesterday.** _____

4. **Tomorrow is Saturday.** _____

5. **I am happy when I try my best!** _____

Wind-Blown Words

The words below have been mixed up by the wind.
Write the letters in their correct order to spell the
words in the word box.

rftea _____

uSnyad _____

Tdrsayuh _____

mrotrwoo _____

phyap _____

veael _____

Word Box

Thursday   tomorrow   happy

after   leave   Sunday

Shadows

Match each word from the word box to the block with its shape. Write the word in the correct shape.

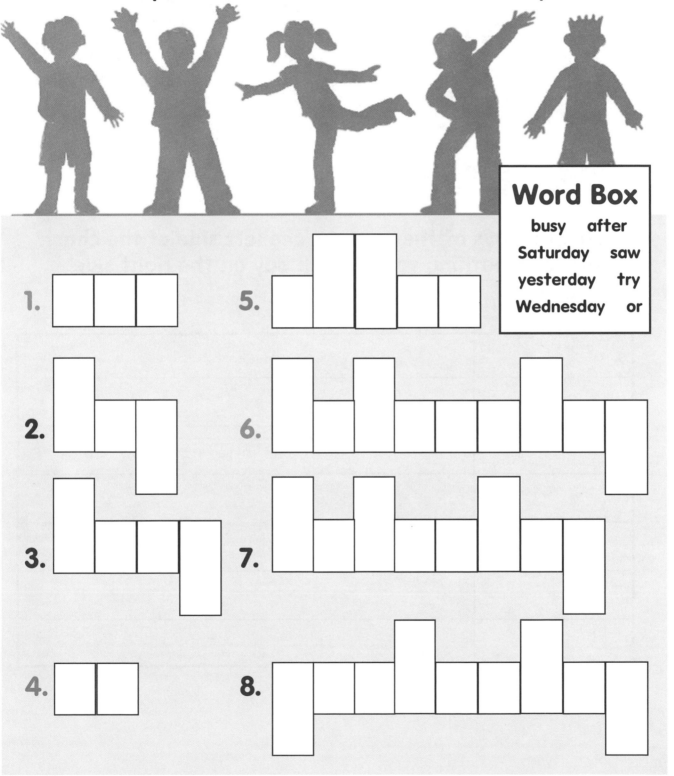

Word Box

busy	after
Saturday	saw
yesterday	try
Wednesday	or

1.

2.

3.

4.

5.

6.

7.

8.

My Busy Week

Write the days of the week on the left side of the chart. Write something you do each day on the right side.

Crossword Fun

**Read the clues and solve using the words in the word box.
Write a letter in each space.**

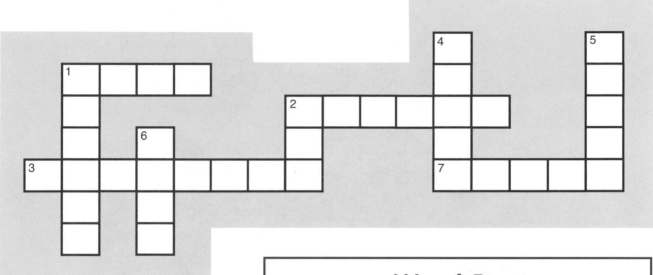

Word Box

leave   every   work   before   happy
Sunday   busy   saw   tomorrow

Across

1. always doing something
2. the first day of the week
3. the day after today
7. each of them

Down

1. the opposite of after
2. to have seen something
4. to go away
5. feeling good
6. to do a job

Word Group 1   15

Flying High

Find your way through the maze by following the words that name the days of the week.

What is your favorite day of the week?

Why? _____

_____

Word Group 1

What's Missing?

In each set of words the same letter is missing. Use the missing letters to write the "mystery word."

1. bef_re

   _r

   w_rk

   The missing letter is ◯

2. Fri_ay

   Satur_ay

   yester_ay

   The missing letter is ◯

3. h_ppy

   le_ve

   s_w

   _fter

   The missing letter is ◯

4. ever_

   Tuesda_

   bus_

   The missing letter is ◯

5. yes_erday

   _hursday

   af_er

   The missing letter is ◯

Mystery Word: ◯ ◯ ◯ ◯ ◯

Silly Sentences

The words in these sentences are all mixed up.
Rewrite each sentence in the correct order.
Remember to use capital letters.

1. Friday to game night every go we the football

_____

2. movie I last saw Wednesday a new

_____

3. Grandmother's leave Tuesday will or Monday we for house

_____

4. dinner work Rob the happy to was do before

_____

Building Blocks

Match each word from the word box to the block with its shape. Write the word in the correct shape.

Word Box

fall	cold	sky
summer		when
grow	spring	snow

1.

2.

3.

4.

5.

6.

7.

8.

Seasons

Write the name of each season in the spaces provided.

_____

_____

_____

_____

_____

_____

_____

_____

Write a story about your favorite season.
Include three things you like about it. What things
do you do during that season?

_____

_____

_____

_____

_____

_____

Contractions

Contractions are two words put together to make a smaller word. One or more letters of one of the words is missing so an apostrophe is used to stand for the missing letters.

Write the two words
that make up each contraction below.

Bonus Question:

What **letter** or **letters** does the apostrophe replace
in each of the contractions below?
Write the **letter** or **letters** in the last column.

1. **hasn't**   has   not   o

2. **isn't**

3. **I'll**

4. **I'm**

5. **don't**

6. **you're**

7. **I've**

Springtime

Fill in each blank with the correct word from the word box.

1. In _____ I can play outside more often.

2. _____ nice to have a friend to play with me.

3. The weather is _____ enough to wear shorts.

4. I can pick a _____ from the garden and give it to my mother.

5. The _____ sometimes fills with rain clouds in the spring.

6. I will need an umbrella _____ the rain falls.

Word Box
flower   spring
warm   sky
when   it's

Write three sentences about what you like to do in spring.

1._____

2._____

3._____

Match-It

Draw a line from the contraction to the two words for which it stands.

don't	I will
I'm	is not
hasn't	do not
you're	I am
I've	I have
isn't	you are
won't	has not
I'll	will not
it's	it is

Write your own sentences using four of these contractions.

_____

_____

_____

_____

Word Group 2   23

Every Which Way

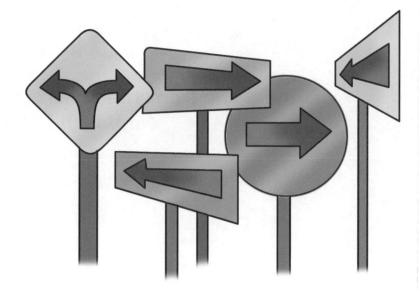

The words below are all scrambled. Write the letters in their correct order to spell the words in the word box.

wogr _____

elwrfo _____

mawr _____

dolc _____

nhew _____

emsrmu _____

Word Box			
summer	cold	flower	grow
	when	warm	

All Through the Year

**Read the clues and solve using the words in the word box.
Write a letter in each space.**

Word Box

winter
fall
spring
snow
summer
cold
flower
grow
sky

Across

1. the season when leaves turn color
2. the hottest season
3. you see this when you look up outside
4. the coldest season
6. what you do as you get older

Down

1. something that blooms
2. the season when leaves are new
3. white, fluffy, cold
5. why you wear a coat

Word Group 2

25

A-Maze-Ing Path

Help the boy get to his friend's house by following the contractions.

What do you like to do with your friend?
Write about a fun thing you did with a friend.

_____

_____

_____

Hidden Words

Find each of the words in the Word Box hidden in the word search below. Words can be vertical, horizontal, backwards, or diagonal.

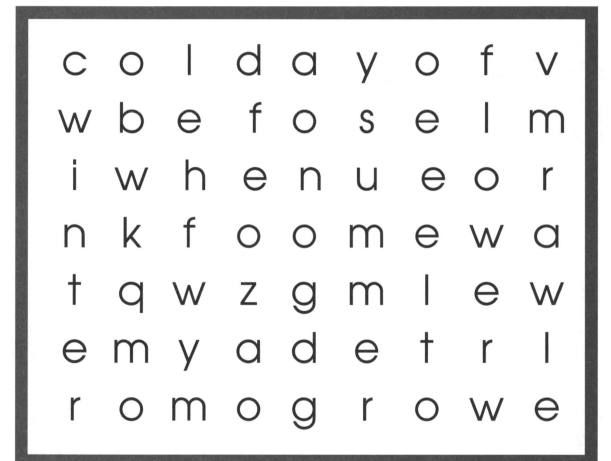

c o l d a y o f v
w b e f o s e l m
i w h e n u e o r
n k f o o m e w a
t q w z g m l e w
e m y a d e t r l
r o m o g r o w e

Word Box

winter	grow	flower	summer
snow	warm	cold	when

Good Times

Write a story that tells what happens during a year,
using words from the word box.

_____

_____

_____

_____

_____

_____

_____

_____

_____

_____

_____

_____

Word Box

spring   I'll   flower   snow   it's   isn't   warm

summer   fall   cold   winter   sky

Word Group 2

ABC Ladder

Put these words on each rung of the ladder in ABC order. Go from top to bottom.

Word Box

those
must
girl
care
all
took
people
whole

Bedtime

Fill in each blank with the correct word from the word box.

1. The _____ in the pink bed is happy.

2. "It is nice to have a _____ like you," she said.

3. "Let's _____ TV and eat popcorn."

4. They both _____ at the funny show.

5. The girls want to stay up _____ night.

6. Soon they will need to go to _____ .

Word Box

sleep	watch	all	friend	laugh	girl

Nouns and Verbs

Nouns are words that name people, places, or things.
Verbs are words that name something you can do.

Write each word
from the word box
on a leaf of the tree
that names its
part of speech

Nouns

Word Box

boy   sleep   brother   took
laugh   friend   woman   children

Verbs

Springtime Flowers

Write the word from the word box that rhymes with all the words on each flower's petals. Write the word on the correct flower pot.

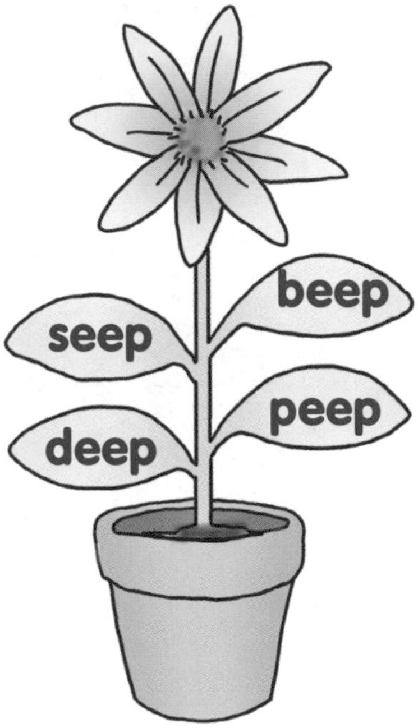

Word Box
all   sleep
took   must

beep
seep
peep
deep

hook
cook
book
look

fall
call
hall
ball

rust
dust
trust
bust

Opposites Attract

**Draw a line
from the word on the
left to its opposite picture on the right.**

 boy

 sleep

 laugh

 girl

Word Group 3  33

My Summer Vacation

Fill in the blanks in the story below with words from the word box.

My _____ is going on a trip. We are riding in our car to another state. My _____ is driving. He likes to fish. We are bringing _____ boat too. My _____ said I could bring a _____, so Kate is coming with us. We will _____ in our tent. What a fun vacation this will be!

Word Box
sleep   our   mother   family   father   friend

Match Game

Draw a line from each picture to the word it describes.

laugh

mother

watch

family

friend

Word Group 3 35

What's the Word?

In each set of words the same
letter is missing.
Use the missing letters to write
the "mystery word."

1. b_y

   w_man

   _ur

   th_se

   The missing letter is ◯

2. Fath_r

   Moth_r

   thos_

   car_

   The missing letter is ◯

3. _atch

   _oman

   The missing letter is ◯

4. gil_

   chi_dren

   fami_y

   peop_e

   The missing letter is ◯

5. brot_er

   c_ildren

   laug_

   watc_

   The missing letter is ◯

Mystery Word: ◯◯◯◯◯

My Family

Use the space below to write a story about something that happened to your family that made you laugh. Use as many words from the word box as you can.

Word Box

brother

father

whole

mother

family

laugh

must

people

children

all

our

"th" Words

When "t" and "h" are together in a word, they make a special sound.

Complete each word below with "th."

1. mo_ _ er

2. _ _ ose

3. bro _ _ er

4. fa _ _ er

Do you know some other "th" words?
Write six of them in the space below.

_____

_____

_____

_____

_____

_____

Color by Number

In the picture below color all of the triangles blue.
Color all of the squares green.
Color all of the circles orange.
Color all of the rhombuses yellow.

Story Order

In each set of 3 pictures, think about the story they tell. Are the pictures in the correct order? Write "first" under what should happen first. Write "second" under the picture that would happen next, and write "third" under the picture that would happen last.

_____   _____   _____

_____   _____   _____

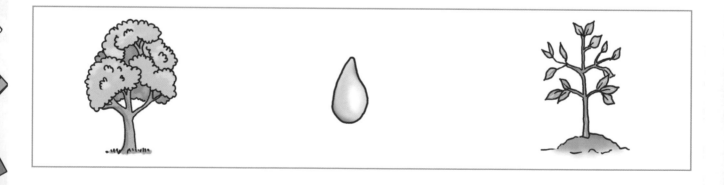

_____   _____   _____

Alphabet Walk

Put these words in ABC order.
Start at the girl's house and end at her school.

Word Box

pretty	school	picture	who	orange	draw	house
	about	build	large	here	look	

Word Group 4 41

Alphabet Soup

Word Box

about

draw

pretty

where

second

long

Use the letters floating in the bowl of soup below to spell some of the words in the word box. You can only use each letter once.

_____   _____

_____   _____

_____   _____

School Years

Use the words from the word box to write a story about the years you have been in school. Write about your first-grade class, your second-grade class, and what you might expect next year in third grade.

_____

_____

_____

_____

Word Box

first	second
third	where
long	school
about	build
here	draw
large	look
who	

_____

_____

_____

_____

_____

Word Group 4 43

Hide 'N Seek Words

Find each of the words in the Word Box, hidden in the word search below. Words can be vertical, horizontal, backwards, or diagonal.

```
p  i  c  t  u  r  e  y  e
w  r  o  r  a  n  g  e  r
i  e  e  g  a  z  g  l  e
n  k  f  t  o  o  l  l  h
e  r  e  h  t  i  h  o  w
b  u  i  l  d  y  w  w  l
r  o  e  g  r  a  l  r  e
```

Word Box

yellow	build
pretty	large
where	who
orange	picture
here	

A Beautiful Picture

Fill in the blanks in the story below with words
from the word box.

My class took their _____ field

trip to the art museum. The museum

is _____ there are many

paintings. We rode to the museum

in a _____ bus. During the

_____ ride we actually drove

by my _____. At the museum

we saw a beautiful _____. The

_____ picture covered an entire wall.

It had a _____ sun in a _____ sky.

It was very _____.

**Word
Box**

large
picture
yellow
blue
long
first
pretty
school
house
where

Can you
draw what
you think the
picture might
look like?

Word Group 4 45

Riddle Me This

Finish the riddles using words from the word box.

1. I am the color of grass, spring leaves, and dollar bills.   I am _____.

2. I am where you learn many things, where you play, and where you see your friends each day.

   I am _____.

3. I am a giant. I am a skyscraper. I am a cruise ship.   I am _____.

4. I am where you will find your family. I am where you sleep at night. I am a safe place.

   I am _____.

5. I am what you do with your eyes. I am what you do when you see things.   I am _____.

Word Box

large

school

look

house

green

Rhyme Time

Draw a line from each picture to the word that rhymes with it.

who

green

house

look

third

Word Group 4  47

Word Math

Write the picture name, then add and subtract letters to make new words.

1.  _____ – h + m = _____

2. 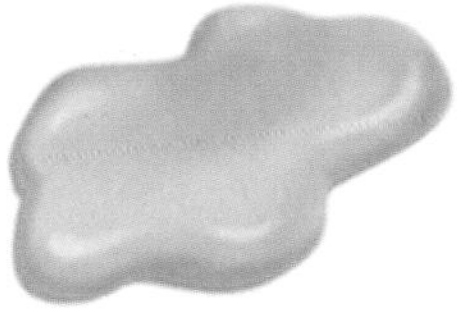 _____ – g – r + s = _____

3.  _____ – s – h = _____

4. 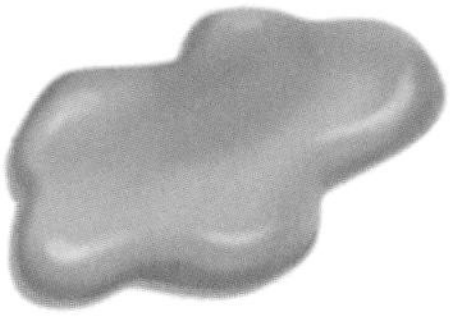 _____ – b – l + t + r = _____

5. 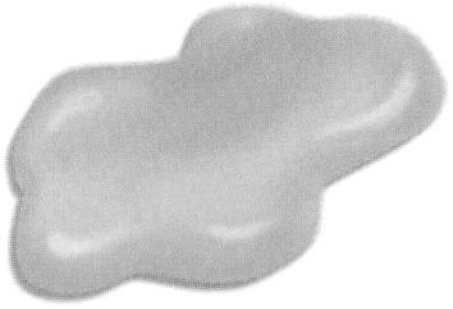 _____ – o = _____

Find It!

Read the clues and solve using the words in the word box. Write a letter in each space.

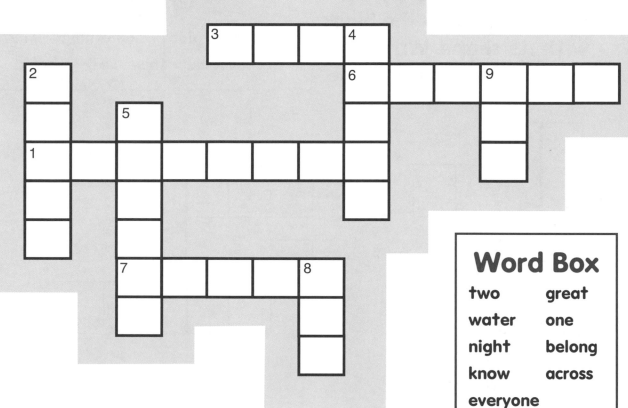

Word Box

two	great
water	one
night	belong
know	across
everyone	

Across

1. all of the people
3. to understand something
6. opposite of down
7. the time of day when you sleep

Down

2. fantastic
4. a clear liquid you drink
5. when you join a group, you
   _____
8. the number after one
9. the first digit in 15

Word Group 5  49

Word Shapes

Match each word from the word box to the block with its shape. Write the word in the correct shape.

1.

2.

3.

4.

5.

6.

7.

8.

Letter Fill-In

In each set of words the same letter is missing. Use the missing letters to write the "mystery word"

1. nigh_

   _wo

   _his

   grea_

   The missing letter is ◯

2. t_o

   kne_

   _hy

   kno_

   The missing letter is ◯

3. gre_t

   _cross

   The missing letter is ◯

4. som_thing

   b_com_

   do_s

   v_ry

   The missing letter is ◯

5. th_ough

   you_

   g_eat

   ac_oss

   The missing letter is ◯

Mystery Word: ◯◯◯◯◯

Word Group 5 51

Summer Camp

Fill in the blanks in the story below with words from the word box.

During the summer I went to Camp Longhorn. I was there for _____ weeks. We spent the _____ in cabins. _____ day we went to the lake. The _____ was cold, but _____ jumped in. Kate ran to _____ in and made a _____ big splash!

"How _____ she do that?" Robbie asked. "Maybe we _____ run like she does."

I had a _____ time at Camp Longhorn. _____ was my favorite year yet. I can't wait to go back next year.

Word Box

jump	everyone	night	two
great	water	very	should
	one	does	this

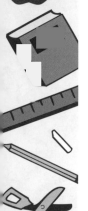

Putting It All Together

Add the smaller words together to form a new word.

1. **some** + **thing** = _____

2. **be** + **come** = _____

3. **every** + **one** = _____

4. **a** + **cross** = _____

5. **be** + **long** = _____

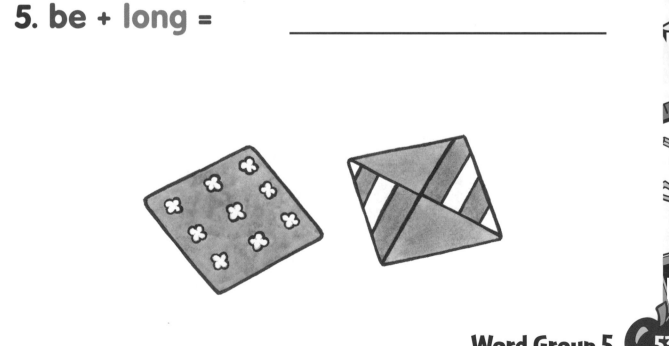

Word Group 5 53

Turtle Watch

Help the baby turtle get to the sea by following the verbs.

Mixed-Up Letters

The words below are all scrambled. Write the letters in their correct order to spell the words in the word box.

wken

_____

duolhs

_____

retwa

_____

bmeeoc

_____

guhorht

_____

ovenerey

_____

oasrcs

_____

Word Box

through	should	become	water
everyone	knew	across	

SHH!

Silent Letters on Board!

Many words include letters that make no sound when you say the word. Match each word below with its silent letters.

1. night   k, w

2. two   gh

3. knew   w

4. great   e

5. know   k

Hide 'N Seek Words

There are smaller words hiding within each of the words below. Can you find them? Write them on the lines.

1. knew _____

2. one _____

3. this _____

4. great _____

5. know _____

6. water _____

7. your _____

Write On!

Use the words in the word box below to write a story about a time you spent the night with a friend.

_____

_____

_____

_____

_____

_____

_____

_____

_____

_____

_____

_____

Word Box	
jump	night
two	this
why	great
one	through
across	water
belong	

Climb the Mountain

Reach the top of the mountain by writing the words from the word box in ABC order. Start at the bottom and go up.

Word Box

again	how
use	heard
until	

Word Group 6   59

© Copyright 2007 by Barron's Educational Series, Inc.

Wild Animals

Write <u>yes</u> or <u>no</u> after each sentence.

1. A lion is a little animal. _____

2. I have heard a tiger roar. _____

3. A zoo is a special place to see wild animals. _____

4. Animals are quiet when they are hunting prey. _____

5. A lion has a loud roar. _____

Write a paragraph about a trip to the zoo.

_____

_____

_____

_____

_____

_____

_____

Mixed-Up Sentences

The words in these sentences are all mixed up. Rewrite each sentence in the correct order. Remember to use capital letters.

1. **home lost little it**

   Bill that dog found

   a brought was and

   _____

   _____

2. **ready now I to am eat right**

   _____

3. **baby because be please the sleeping quiet is**

   _____

4. **would show that to I again like see**

   _____

Opposites

Find the opposites in the word box.
Write them on the lines below.
<u>Hint:</u> Not all the words will have a match.

Word Box

again	use
left	both
brought	loud
right	lost
because	quiet
found	big
what	show
how	little

<u>Word</u>   <u>Opposite</u>

_____   _____

_____   _____

_____   _____

_____   _____

_____   _____

_____   _____

_____   _____

A Surprise Party

Read the story below. Then write three sentences about what happened first, next, and last in the story. The words from this word group are underlined.

My family is getting <u>ready</u> for Ken's <u>special</u> day. Today is his birthday. We are going to give him a surprise party. We invited all of his friends. While Ken is at the <u>show</u>, everyone will come over to our house. Everyone <u>brought</u> presents for Ken. Everything is <u>ready</u>. Now we will wait <u>until</u> Ken comes home. We have to be <u>quiet</u> <u>because</u> we want to surprise Ken. Jerry can hear Ken's car pulling up to the house <u>right</u> now. I hope he hasn't <u>heard</u> us. As he walks in the door, everyone lets out a <u>loud</u> "Happy Birthday!" <u>What</u> a great surprise!

What happened first? _____

_____

What happened next? _____

_____

What happened last? _____

_____

Word Group 6   63

Past and Present

Fill in the blanks below, using the past tense of the underlined word in the first sentence.

1. Today I will <u>bring</u> a sandwich for lunch.

   Yesterday I _____ pizza for lunch.

2. Did you <u>find</u> your sweater?

   I _____ mine under the bed.

3. Did you <u>hear</u> that story on the news?

   My mother _____ about it from her friend.

Word Find

Find each of these words hidden in the word search below. Words can be vertical, horizontal, backwards, or diagonal.

Word Box

both	what	use	how
until	left	again	could
	animal	found	

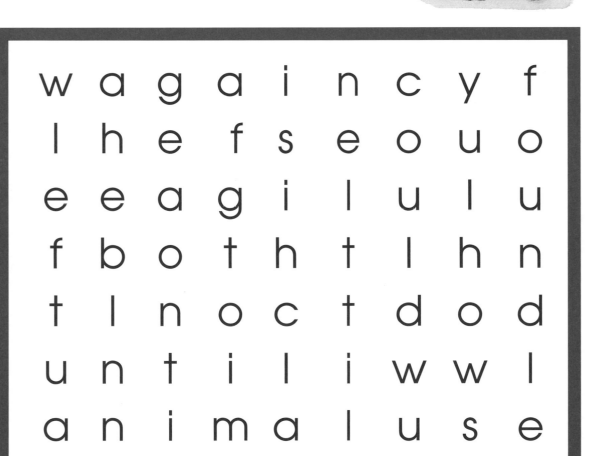

```
w a g a i n c y f
l h e f s e o u o
e e a g i l u l u
f b o t h t l h n
t l n o c t d o d
u n t i l i w w l
a n i m a l u s e
```

Dinosaur Bones

Fill in each blank with the correct word from the word box.

Word Box

both	could
what	use
ready	quiet

1. The children are _____ to see the dinosaur bones.

2. We have to be _____ in the museum.

3. "_____ kind of bones are those?" asked Juan.

4. Our guide asked which animal we thought the bones _____ be from.

5. People would _____ these bones as tools.

6. We got to see _____ dinosaur bones and dinosaur eggs.

Word Shape Match

Match each word from the word box to the block with its shape. Write the word in the correct shape.

Word Box

little	heard	left	could
special	until	quiet	again

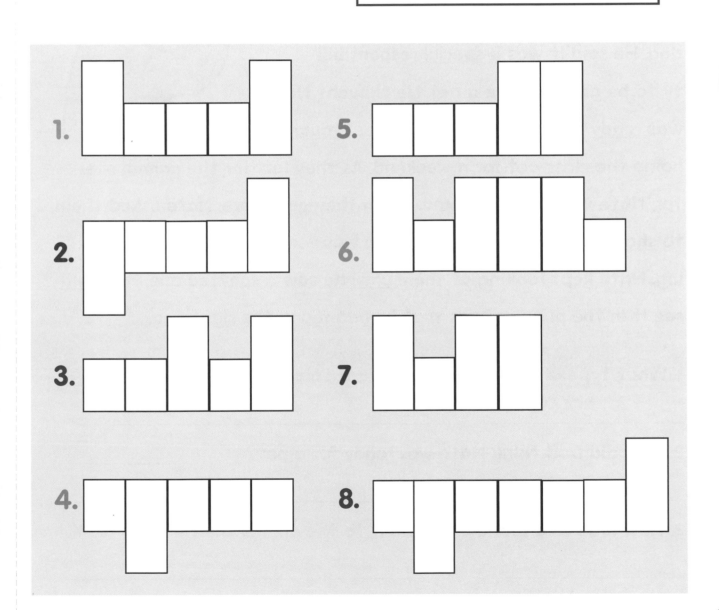

Adopt-A-Pet

Read the story and answer the questions.
The words from this word group are underlined.

One day Nate asked Dad if he <u>could</u> get a dog. Dad wanted to know if Nate was <u>ready</u> to take care of an <u>animal</u>. Dad asked if Nate knew <u>how</u> to take care of a dog. He said it was a <u>special</u> responsibility to be able to have a pet. He thought Nate was <u>ready</u> <u>because</u> Nate sometimes <u>brought</u> home the class pet for a weekend. As they left for the animal shelter, Nate was a <u>little</u> scared. When they got there, Nate asked them to <u>show</u> him the puppies. The room was very <u>loud</u> with all the barking. Nate kept looking at them <u>until</u> he saw a spotted one. He <u>could</u> see it in the puppy's eyes that he had found the right dog.

1. What type of animal did Nate want to adopt? _____

_____

2. Why did Dad think Nate was ready for a pet? _____

_____

3. How did Nate feel as they went to the animal shelter?

_____

4. What does Nate's dog look like? _____

Seeing Double

Each word in the word box below contains double letters. Use these words to create an original story.

Word Box

tooth	carry
follow	been
foot	too

Word Search

Find each of these words hidden in the word search below. Words can be vertical, horizontal, backwards, or diagonal.

```
w e r e r d w y f
l h e f s n o u o
t e i i i u u b t
f u n c h o l d h
t c o o h r d o e
e n t h l a w w r
a l m o s t u n e
```

Word Box

almost   buy   would   other

which   around   shout   down

were   you   since

Ups and Downs

Read the clues and solve using the words in the word box.
Write a letter in each space.

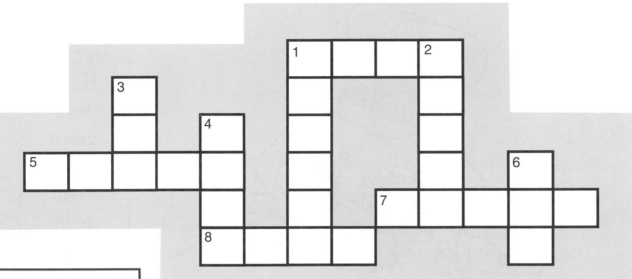

Word Box

foot	close
head	buy
tooth	down
shout	too
follow	

Across

1. a body part with toes
5. near
7. to yell really loudly
8. the opposite of up

Down

1. to walk behind some-one
2. you use this to chew
3. also
4. a body part that sits on your shoulders
6. to pay for something

Scrambled Letters

The words below are all scrambled. Write the letters in their correct order to spell the words in the word box.

rtoeh _____

hihwc _____

cnies _____

ebne _____

veha _____

staoml _____

udolw _____

Did You Lose Something?

In each set of words the same letter is missing. Use the missing letters to write the "mystery word."

3. a_ound

we_e

The missing letter is ◯

1. f_ll_w

cl_se

d_wn

y_u

The missing letter is ◯

2. _ave

s_out

toot_

_ead

The missing letter is ◯

4. almos_

foo_

shou_

_oo_h

The missing letter is ◯

5. h_ad

clos_

hav_

sinc_

The missing letter is ◯

Mystery Word: ◯ ◯ ◯ ◯ ◯

Word Group 7 73

Homophones

Homophones are words that sound alike, but are spelled differently. Draw a line to match the homophones on the leaves below.

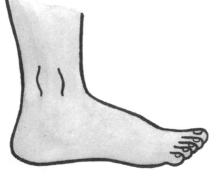

Picture Match

Draw a line from each picture to the word it describes.

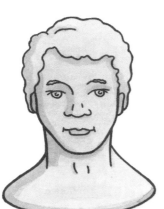

head

tooth

buy

carry

foot

The Shopping Trip

Fill in the blanks in the story below with words from the word box. You can use the same word more than once.

Bill and Sue went to the mall. They wanted to _____ some new clothes for school. Bill saw two shirts that he liked, but he couldn't decide _____ one to get. He decided to _____ them both. Sue found some shirts, _____. They continued to walk _____ to see what _____ clothes they could _____. Bill and Sue bought many nice things for school. After they had _____ shopping for two hours, they decided to _____ their bags to the car and go home. Now they are ready for the first day of school.

Word Box

buy	around
were	been
other	too
carry	which

Build-A-Word

Add and subtract the
letters to
form new words.

1. frown - fr + d = _____

2. out + sh = _____

3. shave - s = _____

4. should - sh + w = _____

5. your - r = _____

The Soccer Game

Read the story below. Then write three sentences about what happened first, next, and last in the story. The words from this word group are underlined.

Gus had a soccer game today. His team had won <u>almost</u> all of their games, so they <u>were</u> in the tournament. Gus had to <u>carry</u> the ball out to the field. He kicked it with his <u>foot</u> to start the game. The <u>other</u> team ran after him. Everyone was <u>around</u> him. He didn't know <u>which</u> way to run, so he decided to <u>follow</u> his teammate, Sam, <u>down</u> the field. As they got <u>close</u> to the goal, Gus heard Sam <u>shout</u>, "Kick it!" Gus kicked the ball into the air and Sam hit it with his <u>head</u> into the net. "<u>You</u> scored!" Gus said to Sam. They <u>were</u> happy because they helped to win the game.

What happened first? _____

What happened next? _____

What happened last? _____

Step Up to It!

**Climb the stairs by writing
the words from the word box in ABC order.
Start at the bottom and go up.**

Word Box

story	once
just	between
for	are
upon	

"Once Upon a Time"

Use the words from the word box to write a fantasy story. Your story must start with the words "Once upon a time..."

Word Box

start	finish
book	just
upon	write
put	some

_____

_____

_____

_____

_____

_____

_____

_____

_____

_____

_____

_____

_____

Word Blocks

Write the letters that fit in each
block to spell a word from the word box.

Word Box

start	finish	book	just
upon	write	put	some

1.

2.

3.

4.

5.

6.

7.

8.

Jumbled Sentences

The words in these sentences are all mixed up. Rewrite each sentence in the correct order. Remember to use capital letters.

1. horses I read about just book a

_____

2. decide the soft cream Paul sundae really the can't

and between ice

_____

_____

3. upon will story time a I with start my once

_____

4. finish you to going are dinner your

_____

Mystery Word

In each set of words the same letter is missing. Use the missing letters to write the "mystery word."

1. f_r
   up_n
   s_me
   g_es
   The missing letter is ◯

2. _ead
   answe_
   f_om
   w_ite
   The missing letter is ◯

3. alwa_s
   reall_
   The missing letter is ◯

4. an_wer
   goe_
   _tart
   fini_h
   The missing letter is ◯

5. be_ween
   sof_
   jus_
   pu_
   The missing letter is ◯

Mystery Word:

◯ ◯ ◯ ◯ ◯

Word Group 8 83

Library Time

Fill in each blank with the correct word from the word box.

Word Box

always

goes

soft

put

book

for

some

once

1. I went to the library to check out a _____ .

2. I _____ my books on the counter.

3. Julie _____ sits on the big, _____ pillow on the floor when she reads.

4. My class _____ to the library _____ a week.

5. Mr. Baker helps us look _____ books.

6. I got _____ books about ballet.

Solve the Riddle

Finish the riddles using words from the word box.

Word Box

soft   read

book   write

answer

1. I can be soft or hard. I can be funny or sad. I am something you read. I am a _____ .

2. I am something you can do. You can use a pencil to do this. You can do this on paper or in the sand. I am _____ .

3. I can be correct. I can be wrong. I solve problems. I am an _____ .

4. I feel good. I can be a blanket. I can be a kitten. I can be a sweater. I am _____ .

5. You can do this anywhere. I help you learn new things. You are doing it right now! I am _____ .

Match Up

Draw a line from each picture to the word it describes.

soft

read

write

finish

book

The Race

Read the story and answer the questions.
The words from this word group are underlined.

Today is Thanksgiving Day. There is <u>always</u> a big race on this day. It is called the Turkey Trot. <u>Some</u> people run every year, but today will be my first time to run. The <u>start</u> is at the park and the <u>finish</u> line is at the zoo. I <u>put</u> on my shoes and now I am <u>just</u> waiting for the gun to go off to <u>start</u> the race. I am <u>really</u> nervous, but once I <u>start</u> running I'll be fine. I am going to run over 3 miles!

1. What special day is it? _____

2. What is the name of the race? _____

3. Where will the race start? _____

4. Where is the finish line? _____

5. How far will he run? _____

Movie Night

Look at the picture below and write a story about it.
Use the words in the word box to help you.

_____

_____

_____

_____

_____

_____

_____

_____

_____

_____

_____

_____

_____

_____

_____

_____

Word Box

always   between

put   from   really

are   for   goes

Star Bright, Star Light

Find your way through the night sky by following the stars with "th" words on them and see a constellation appear.

"th" words

another	thank
thought	their
teeth	think

Can You See Them?

Find each of these words hidden in the word search below. Words can be vertical, horizontal, backwards, or diagonal.

Word Box

by	off	over	soon
any	guess	only	
please	ask	sorry	
out	said		

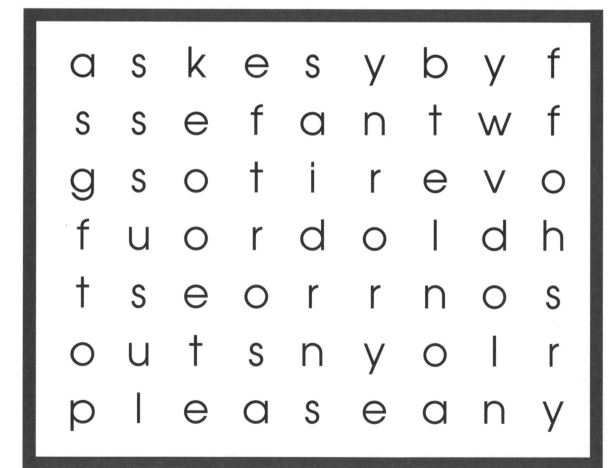

a s k e s y b y f
s s e f a n t w f
g s o t i r e v o
f u o r d o l d h
t s e o r r n o s
o u t s n y o l r
p l e a s e a n y

Manners

Fill in each blank with the correct word from the word box.

Word Box

thank	sorry
please	only
wear	ask

1. At the table I always _____ for

   something when I want it instead of grabbing.

2. I say _____ when I ask for more.

3. I _____ take the amount of food I know

   I can eat, never more.

4. You should not _____ a hat at the table.

5. If I spill something I say _____ and offer

   to clean it up.

6. Don't forget to say _____ you at the end

   of the meal.

Word Group 9 91

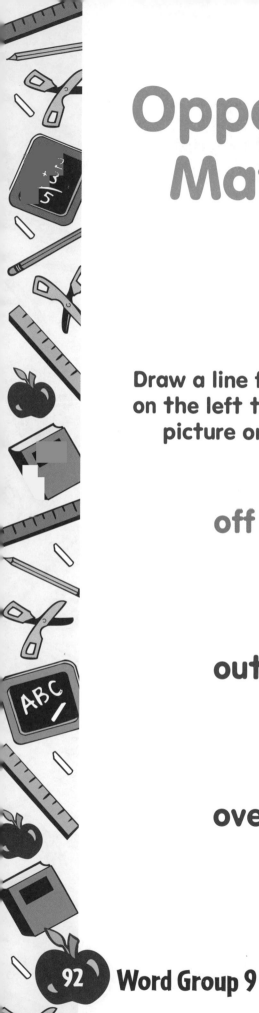

Opposite Match

Draw a line from the word on the left to its opposite picture on the right.

off

out

over

Word Recipes

Follow the **recipes** to form new words.

1. **Start with the word many. Take off the m. The new word is _____ .**

2. **Start with the word tooth. Replace the oo with ee. The new word is _____ .**

3. **Start with the word mess. Replace the m with gu. The new word is _____ .**

4. **Start with the word mother. Replace the m with an. The new word is _____ .**

5. **Start with the word though. Add a t at the end. The new word is _____ .**

6. **Start with the word thank. Replace the a with i. The new word is _____ .**

Word Group 9   93

Once Upon a Rhyme

Draw a line from each picture to the word that rhymes with it.

soon

think

now

their

by

Solve It!

Read the clues and solve using the words in the word box. Write a letter in each space.

Across

1. the opposite of under
3. an idea or notion
7. right away
8. what you do with clothes

Down

2. you use these to chew
4. the opposite of in
5. _____ you!
6. the opposite of later
7. how you feel when you've done something wrong

Word Box

sorry   over

soon   now

out   teeth

wear   thank

thought

Word Group 9   95

Broken Words

The words below are all scrambled. Write the letters in their correct order to spell the words in the word box.

Word Box
their   thought   said   guess
another   any

suegs   _____

tughtoh   _____

yan   _____

dsia   _____

eriht   _____

rotanhe   _____

Snow Time

Read the story below. Then write three sentences about what happened first, next, and last in the story. The words from this word group are underlined.

The snow was falling and Sue called to <u>ask</u> Mary to come <u>over</u> to play. They were going to go out in the snow, so they had to <u>wear</u> warm coats. <u>Soon</u> <u>their</u> friends, Matt and Jack, came <u>by</u> to play. Jack <u>thought</u> it would be fun to build a snowman. They built a big snow-man, but they couldn't find any sticks for arms. They asked Sue's mom if they could <u>please</u> use two wooden spoons for the arms. <u>Now</u> they could finish <u>their</u> snowman. <u>By</u> <u>now</u> everyone's <u>teeth</u> were chattering, so they knew it was time to go in for hot chocolate and cookies.

What happened first? _____

_____

What happened next? _____

_____

What happened last? _____

_____

Word Group 9 97

Look Closely

There are smaller words hiding within each of the words below. Can you find them? Write them on the lines.

1. **another** _____

2. **only** _____

3. **wear** _____

4. **thank** _____

5. **said** _____

6. **off** _____

7. **please** _____

Building Blocks

Write the letters that fit in each block to spell a word from the word box.

Word Box

walk	much	none	piece
either	sing	talk	there

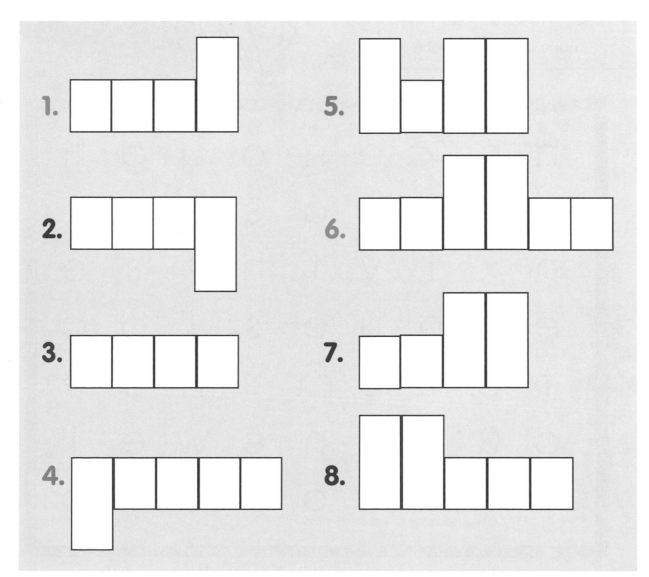

1.

2.

3.

4.

5.

6.

7.

8.

Flying High Word Search

Find each of these words hidden in the word search below. Words can be vertical, horizontal, backwards, or diagonal.

Word Box

enough   more   never
next   toward   was   new
none   these   piece

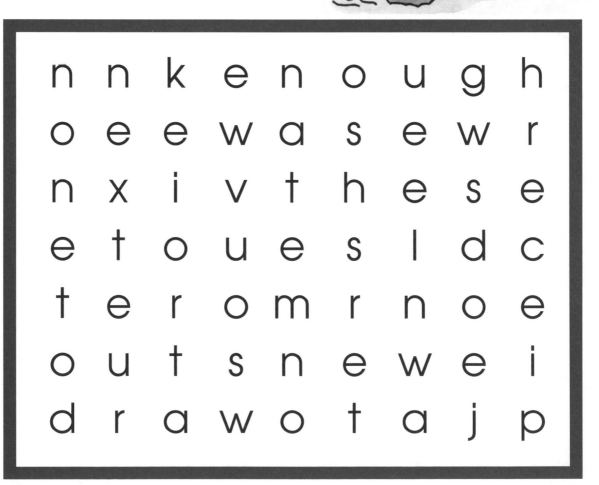

```
n  n  k  e  n  o  u  g  h
o  e  e  w  a  s  e  w  r
n  x  i  v  t  h  e  s  e
e  t  o  u  e  s  l  d  c
t  e  r  o  m  r  n  o  e
o  u  t  s  n  e  w  e  i
d  r  a  w  o  t  a  j  p
```

Flying High

Write the words from the word box on the kite's tail in ABC order. Start at the top and go down.

Word Box

either	many	need
none	enough	more
	paper	

Rhyming Maze

Help the fireman get the cat out of the tree. Follow the words that rhyme with the words in the word box.

seed

few

talk

ring

please

where

door

Word Box

more	there
these	sing
walk	new
need	

Friends

Read the story and answer the questions. The words from this word group are underlined.

Scott and Eddie are friends. <u>They</u> live <u>next</u> door to each other. Today <u>they</u> are going to take a <u>walk</u> to visit the <u>new</u> library. <u>There</u> are <u>many</u> <u>new</u> books. Eddie will <u>need</u> to get a book about animals for his report. Scott shows him books about elephants and tigers. Eddie doesn't want <u>either</u> of those books. <u>They</u> <u>walk</u> <u>toward</u> the section on fish where Eddie finds a book about sharks. That is the book for him. As <u>they</u> leave the library, Eddie and Scott <u>talk</u> about it. <u>They</u> will go back again soon.

1. Who are friends? _____

_____

2. What is the topic of Eddie's report? _____

_____

3. What animal does Eddie choose for his report? _____

_____

Word Group 10 103

Keeping Cool

The words below are all scrambled. Write the letters in their correct order to spell the words in the word box.

Word Box

enough	much	never
piece	these	paper

etseh _____

envre _____

hmcu _____

ugoehn _____

eicpe _____

rapep _____

Things I Can Do

Write a story about things you can do. Use the words in the word box to help you. Some of the words are verbs. Verbs are action words.

Word Box

either	many
paper	talk
sing	walk
much	never
need	

_____

_____

_____

_____

_____

_____

_____

_____

_____

_____

Word Group 10 105

Missing Vowels

Fill in the missing vowels to form words from this word group.

1. n_w   _____

2. s_ng   _____

3. w_s   _____

4. w_lk   _____

5. p_p_r   _____

6. t_w_rd   _____

Riddle Rhymes

Finish these rhyming riddles using words from the word box.

Word Box

talk

more

need

walk

new

1. I rhyme with seed. When you just have to have it, it's something you _____ .

2. I rhyme with door. When you don't have enough you always want _____ .

3. I rhyme with walk. When you have something to say use your mouth and _____ .

4. I rhyme with chalk. You use your legs when you want to _____ .

5. I rhyme with few. If I'm not old, I must be _____ .

Word Group 10 107

Fill-Ins

Fill in each blank with the correct word from the word box.

Word Box

enough   these   was
none   much   next

1. I can never get _____ time to play outside.

2. _____ time I will ask for orange juice instead of apple juice.

3. I _____ absent from school because of a sore throat.

4. I really like _____ beautiful flowers.

5. _____ of those shoes fit.

6. I always eat too _____ birthday cake at parties.

Rodeo Round-Up

Find the words in the word box that are nouns (words that name a person, place, or thing) and write them inside the cowboy's rope.

Word Box

water   don't   house   animal

across   tooth   finish

picture   father   third   jump

night   green   book

Mixed Word Group  109

Sail On!

Write the words from the word box on the sailboats in alphabetical order.

Word Box

soft   who   follow   piece
thought   either

Mixed Word Group

Summer Fun

Read the clues and solve using the words in the word box.
Write a letter in each space.

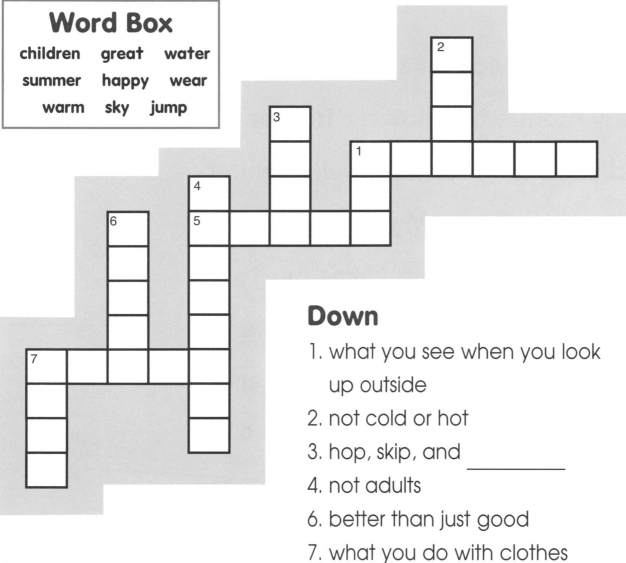

Word Box

children great water
summer happy wear
warm sky jump

Down

1. what you see when you look up outside
2. not cold or hot
3. hop, skip, and _____
4. not adults
6. better than just good
7. what you do with clothes

Across

1. the hottest season of the year
5. the opposite of sad
7. you drink this when you are hot

Mixed Word Group 111

Happy Mother's Day

Read the story. Unscramble the words in bold letters to spell words from the word lists. Write the words below.

Tdayo is **Mother's Day.** I bought
my mom **emos** flowers for her
clisepa day. **Tyhe** are **wlyole,** her
favorite color. My mom **osed** so
umhc for me. She takes me to
soccer practice. She helps me
with my homework. She listens
to me **rdea.** My mom is also a
good cook. She makes the most
delicious barbeque ribs. The
best thing **batuo** my mom,
though, is that she gives me the
best hugs in the world!

_____

_____

_____

_____

_____

_____

_____

_____

Follow the Trail

Find each of the words in the Word Box, hidden in the word search below. Words can be vertical, horizontal, backwards, or diagonal.

```
b  p  l  e  a  s  e  g  f
o  l  a  l  a  u  g  h  o
n  e  u  v  t  h  i  s  l
n  e  v  e  r  u  o  y  l
t  e  r  o  m  u  s  t  o
f  r  o  m  n  e  w  e  w
d  n  o  c  e  s  a  j  p
```

Word Box

blue	second
follow	must
this	never
please	laugh
your	from

Words Within Words

Find the smaller words that are hidden within the larger word. Write them on the lines.

something _____

Saturday _____

orange _____

great _____

where _____

Lost and Found

The letters in the words below are lost. Put them back together to form the words in the word box.

gthin _____

aangi _____

uldib _____

etriw _____

roeth _____

ognehu _____

Word Box

again	write	other
night	enough	build

Mixed Word Group  115

Hooray for Kate!

Read the story below and fill in each blank with
a word from the word box.

It was a great day for Kate.
She had been working all week
on a story for her teacher, Mr.
Van. It was a story about a boy
who lived near the water. He
would swim with the fish.
He left food for the deer. He
watched the birds build nests for their babies. Kate even drew
a picture to go with her story. She was proud of her work. Mr.
Van liked her story too. He read it
to the class and showed everyone
her picture. She got a big star on
her paper for all of her hard work.

Word Box

great   water   read   story
about   would   left   build
their   picture   everyone   paper

1. Kate wrote a _____.

2. It was _____ a boy who lived near the _____.

3. She also drew a _____ to go with her story.

4. Mr. Van _____ her story to the class.

5. He showed _____ her picture.

Mixed Word Group

It's Magic!

Draw lines to match the first syllable of each word
to the second syllable.

sum   ther

pa   mer

pic   ture

fa   per

Mixed Word Group   117

Seasons

Fill in each blank of the poem with a rhyming word from the word box.

Word Box

school   snow   show

grow   one   sky

Every year they come and go.

The seasons change; the flowers _____.

In spring the kites are flying high.

They look so pretty in the _____.

In winter when the cold winds blow,

The ground is covered with ice and _____.

All the outdoor summer fun,

Makes that season my favorite _____.

In the fall when the weather turns cool,

That's the time to head back to _____.

Every year they come and go.

The seasons put on their special _____.

Paper or Plastic?

A noun is a word that names a person, place, or thing. A verb is an action word. It describes something you can do.

Write each word in the word box in the correct bag.

Nouns

Verbs

Word Box

sleep   flower   picture

heard   buy   ask   paper

jump   night   mother

Mixed Word Group 119

Picture/ Word Match

Draw a line from each picture to the word it describes.

sing

night

school

flower

soft

ABC Challenge

Write the words below in ABC order. Be careful,
they all start with the same letter!

Word Box

before   busy   boy
by   brother   blue

1. _____

2. _____

3. _____

4. _____

5. _____

6. _____

Mixed Word Group   121

Same, but Different

**Many words sound alike, but are spelled differently.
They are called homophones.**

Word Box	
some	one
hear	sense
flower	piece

Read each word in the word box.
Write it next to its homophone below.

1. flour _____

2. hear _____

3. sum _____

4. won _____

5. peace _____

6. cents _____

Fall Days

Write the words from the leaves on the tree on the bag with its rhyming word.

Artistic Crossword

Read the clues and solve using the words in the word box. Write a letter in each space.

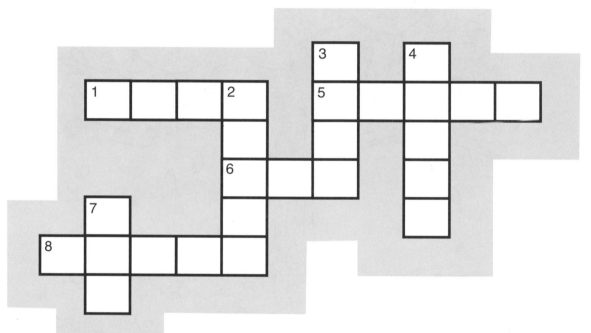

Across

1. completes a task
5. to go away
6. 7 — 6 = ?
8. not noisy

Down

2. to yell
3. the color of the sky
4. to take something from one place to another in your arms
7. the opposite of in

Word Box

leave   blue

quiet   shout

out   one

does   carry

Word Find

Find each of the words in the word box hidden in the word search below. Words can be vertical, horizontal, backwards, or diagonal.

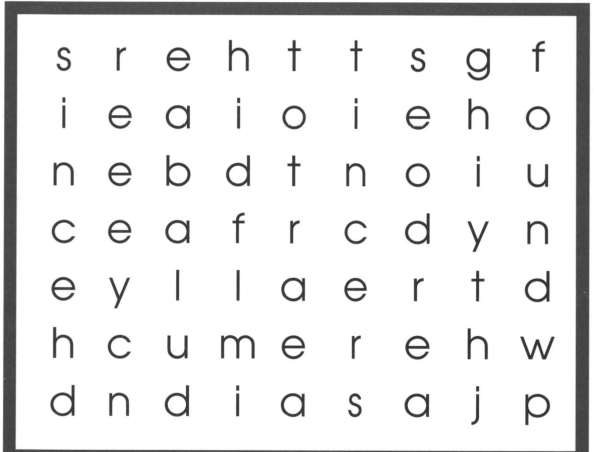

s	r	e	h	t	t	s	g	f
i	e	a	i	o	i	e	h	o
n	e	b	d	t	n	o	i	u
c	e	a	f	r	c	d	y	n
e	y	l	l	a	e	r	t	d
h	c	u	m	e	r	e	h	w
d	n	d	i	a	s	a	j	p

Word Box

where	found	really	since
much	said	does	today

Mixed Word Group 125

At the Store

Read the story and answer the questions.
The words from the word groups are underlined.

Andy and his <u>mother</u> <u>were</u> at the grocery store. Andy liked going to the store with his mom. <u>They</u> went <u>every</u> week. He <u>always</u> helped her plan <u>what</u> <u>they</u> <u>would</u> eat, then he <u>would</u> help her find things at the store. <u>Today</u> <u>they</u> <u>were</u> looking for fruit to make a pie. <u>They</u> <u>were</u> going to <u>use</u> apples and peaches in the pie. Andy liked apple pie and his <u>father</u> liked peach pie, so <u>they</u> decided to use <u>both</u>! Andy picked <u>out</u> <u>some</u> nice red apples and <u>some</u> juicy peaches to use. He <u>put</u> them on the scale to weigh them. Andy's <u>mother</u> paid for the fruit and then <u>they</u> went home to make pie. That <u>night</u> at dinner <u>they</u> ate the pie and it <u>was</u> <u>great</u>!

1. Where are Andy and his mother? _____

2. What kind of fruit were they going to buy? _____

3. What are they going to make? _____

126 **Mixed Word Group**

Color by Words

Color all the spaces with words that name the days of week in red. Color all the spaces with words that are adjectives (describing words) in pink. Color all the spaces with contractions purple. Color all the spaces with words that name colors in that color.

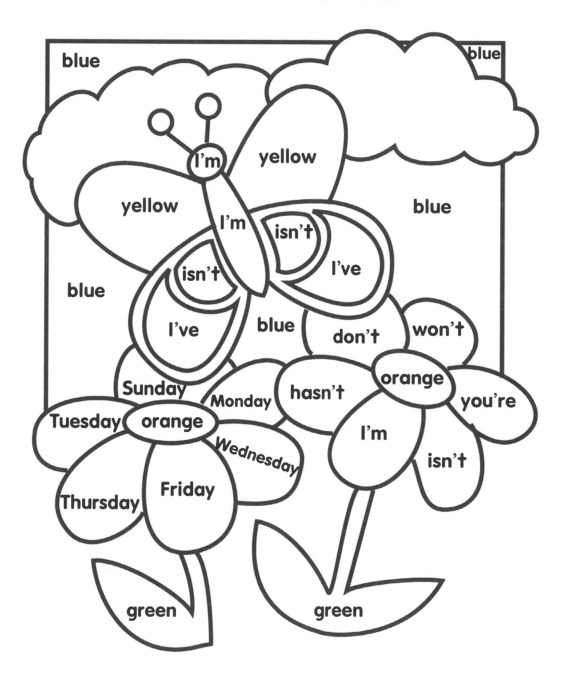

Mixed Word Group 127

Can You Put These Words Back Together Again?

The words below are broken. Put them back together to form the words in the word box.

mowna _____

lryeal _____

ths'na _____

ecilsap _____

rwsaen _____

hhgturo _____

Word Box
special	through
hasn't	woman
answer	really

Yellowstone

Read the story. Unscramble the words in bold letters to spell words from the word lists. Write the words below.

_____

_____

_____

_____

_____

_____

_____

_____

_____

_____

_____

_____

Have you ever **nebe** to Yellowstone Park? It is a **vrye** big park and **eerth** are **amyn** things to do. You can hike in the mountains along trails that wind **rhgotuh** the trees. You have to **erwa** bells as you **wlka** so **yeht** will ring and scare away the bears! Yellowstone has many places **hewer** the earth's heat is so **lseoc** to the ground that the **tware** steams and bubbles. **Smeo** of the hot pools are so hot they are boiling! Old Faithful is the most famous geyser in the park. It gets so hot that the water erupts out of it **sotmla** **eeryv** hour. You can fish in Yellowstone Lake and the Yellowstone River. Gibbon Falls and the Lower Falls are **otw** beautiful waterfalls in the park. You will be able to see all of **etseh** things, and **hmcu** **orem**, when you visit Yellowstone Park.

Mixed Word Group 129

Word Group 1

Answer Key

Page 9 — ABC Train

after, busy, every, happy, or, saw, today, work

Page 10 — Be a Word Detective

```
m o n d a y o f t
w b e f o r e r r
o q l e a v e i y
r k f l e b f d h
k q p z g e l a o
n m y a d o t y l
t o m o r r o w e
```

Page 11 — All About Me

yes, yes, varies, varies, yes

Page 12 — Wind-Blown Words

after, Sunday, Thursday, tomorrow, happy, leave

Page 13 — Shadows

1. saw 2. try 3. busy 4. or 5. after 6. Wednesday 7. Saturday 8. yesterday

Page 14 — My Busy Week

Sunday, Monday, Tuesday, Wednesday, Thursday, Friday, Saturday

Page 15 — Crossword Fun

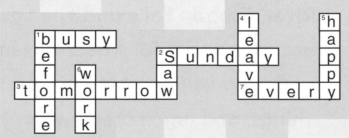

Page 16 — Flying High

Page 17 — What's Missing

    1. o 2. d 3. a 4. y 5. t   Mystery Word: today

Page 18 — Silly Sentences

    1. We go to the football game every Friday night.

    2. I saw a new movie last Wednesday.

    3. We will leave for Grandmother's house Monday or Tuesday.

    4. Rob was happy to do the work before dinner.

Word Group 2

Answer Key

Page 19 — Building Blocks

    1. cold 2. sky 3. snow 4. grow 5. when 6. summer 7. fall 8. spring

Page 20 — Seasons
From top to bottom:

spring, summer, fall, winter

Page 21 — Contractions

has	not	o
is	not	o
I	will	wi
I	am	a
do	not	o
you	are	a
I	have	ha

Page 22 — Springtime

    1. spring 2. It's 3. warm 4. flower 5. sky 6. when

Page 23 — Match-It

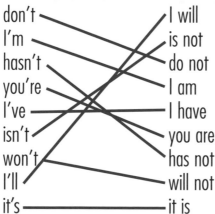

don't	I will
I'm	is not
hasn't	do not
you're	I am
I've	I have
isn't	you are
won't	has not
I'll	will not
it's	it is

Page 24 — Every Which Way

grow, flower, warm, cold, when, summer

Word Group 2

Page 25 — All Through the Year

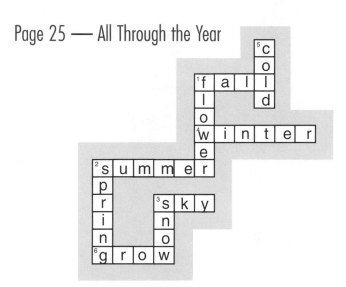

Page 26 — A-Maze-Ing Path

Page 27 — Hidden Words

Word Group 3

Answer Key

Page 29 — ABC Ladder

all, care, girl, must, people, those, took, whole

Page 30 — Bedtime

1. girl, 2. friend, 3. watch, 4. laugh, 5. all, 6. sleep

Page 31 — Nouns and Verbs

verbs—laugh, sleep, took

nouns—boy, brother, children, woman, friend

Page 32 — Springtime Flowers

Page 33 — Opposites Attract

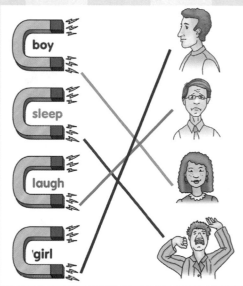

Page 34 — My Summer Vacation

family, father, our, mother, friend, sleep

Page 35 — Match Game

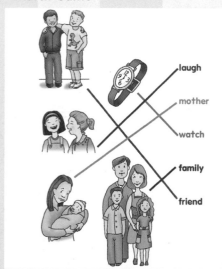

Page 36 — What's the Word?

1. o, 2. e, 3. w, 4. l, 5. h   Mystery word: whole

Page 38 — "th" Words

1. mother 2. those 3. brother 4. father

Word Group 3  135

Word Group 4

Answer Key

Page 39 — Color by Number

Page 40 — Story Order

Page 41 — Alphabet Walk

who
school
pretty
picture
orange
look
large
house
here
draw
build
about

Page 42 — Alphabet Soup

about, second, long, where

Page 44 — Hide 'N Seek Words

Page 45 — A Beautiful Picture

first, where, school, long, house, picture, large, yellow, blue, pretty

Page 46 — Riddle Me This

green, school, large, house, look

Page 47 — Rhyme Time

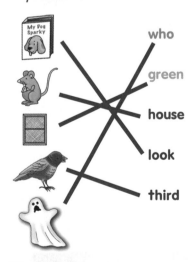

who

green

house

look

third

Page 48 — Word Math

1. house − h + m = mouse
2. green − g − r + s = seen
3. school − s − h = cool
4. blue − b − l + t + r = true
5. orange − o = range

Word Group 4 137

Word Group 5

Answer Key

Page 49 — Find It!

Page 50 — Word Shapes

1. this 2. why 3. your 4. does 5. very 6. become 7. something 8. should

Page 51 — Letter Fill-In

1. t 2. w 3. a 4. e 5. r   Mystery Word: water

Page 52 — Summer Camp

two, night, one, water, everyone, jump, very, does, should, great, this

Page 53 — Putting It All Together

1. something
2. become
3. everyone
4. across
5. belong

Page 54 — Turtle Watch

Page 55 — Mixed-Up Letters

knew, should, water, become, through, everyone, across

Page 56 — SHH! Silent Letters on Board!

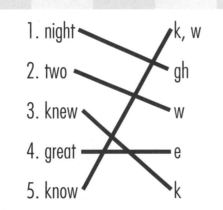

1. night   k, w

2. two   gh

3. knew   w

4. great   e

5. know   k

Page 57 — Hide 'N Seek Words

1. new 2. on 3. is, his 4. eat, at 5. no, now 6. ate, at 7. you, our

Word Group 6

Answer Key

Page 59 — Climb the Mountain

use

until

how

heard

again

Page 60 — Wild Animals

    1. no 2. varies 3. yes 4. yes 5. yes

Page 61 — Mixed-Up Sentences

    1. Bill found a little dog that was lost and brought it home.

    2. I am ready to eat right now.

    3. Please be quiet because the baby is sleeping.

    4. I would like to see that show again.

Page 62 — Opposites

    left/right, loud/quiet, lost/found, big/little

Page 63 — A Surprise Party

    First — Everyone comes with presents.

    Second — Ken's car pulls up.

    Third — Everyone yells "Happy Birthday!"

Word Group 6

Page 64 — Past and Present

       1. brought

       2. found

       3. heard

Page 65 — Word Find

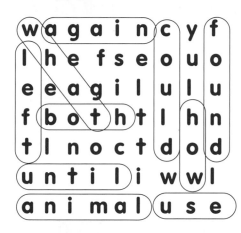

Page 66 — Dinosaur Bones

       1. ready 2. quiet 3. what 4. could 5. use 6. both

Page 67 — Word Shape Match

       1. heard 2. quiet 3. until 4. again 5. could 6. little 7. left 8. special

Page 68 — Adopt-A-Pet

       1. Nate wanted to adopt a dog.

       2. Nate had taken care of the class pet over the weekend.

       3. Nate was a little scared.

       4. His dog is spotted.

Word Group 7

Answer Key

Page 70 — Word Search

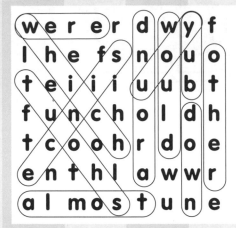

Page 71 — Ups and Downs

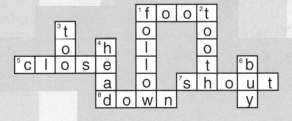

Page 72 — Scrambled Letters

other, which, since, been, have, almost, would

Page 73 — Did You Lose Something?

1. o 2. h 3. r 4. t 5. e Mystery Word: other

Page 74 — Homophones

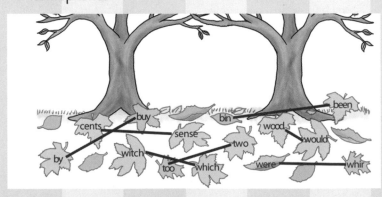

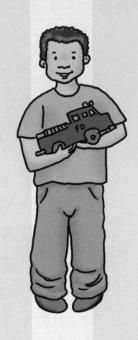

Page 75 — Picture Match

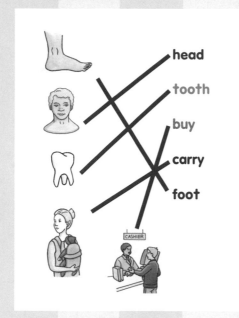

Page 76 — The Shopping Trip

buy, which, buy, too, around, other, buy, been, carry

Page 77 — Build-A-Word

1. down 2. shout 3. have 4. would 5. you

Page 78 — The Soccer Game

First — Gus carried the ball onto the field.

Second — Gus dribbled the ball down the field.

Third — Gus scored a goal.

Word Group 7   143

Word Group 8
Answer Key

Page 79 — Step Up to It!

upon
story
once
just
for
between
are

Page 81 — Word Blocks

    1. some   2. put   3. upon   4. just   5. book   6. finish   7. start   8. write

Page 82 — Jumbled Sentences

    1. I just read a book about horses.

    2. Paul really can't decide between the soft ice cream and the sundae.

    3. I will start my story with once upon a time.

    4. Are you going to finish your dinner?

Page 83 — Mystery Word

    1. o   2. r   3. y   4. s   5. t   Mystery Word: story

Page 84 — Library Time

      1. book 2. put 3. always, soft 4. goes, once 5. for 6. some

Page 85 — Solve the Riddle

      book, write, answer, soft, read

Page 86 — Match Up

Page 87 — The Race

    1. It is Thanksgiving Day.

    2. The race is called the Turkey Trot.

    3. The race will start at the park.

    4. The finish line is at the zoo.

    5. He will run over 3 miles.

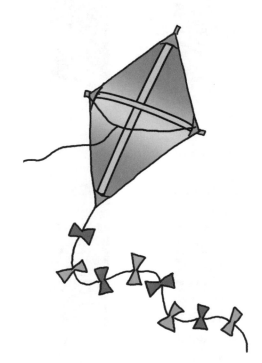

Word Group 8

Word Group 9

Page 89 — Star Bright, Star Light

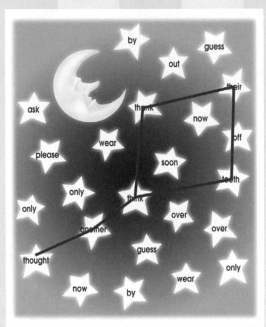

Page 90 — Can You See Them?

Page 91 — Manners

1. ask 2. please 3. only 4. wear 5. sorry 6. thank

Page 92 — Opposite Match

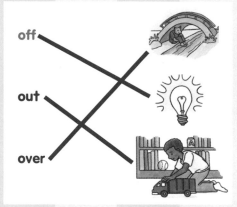

Page 93 — Word Recipes

1. any 2. teeth 3. guess 4. another 5. thought 6. think

Page 94 — Once Upon a Rhyme

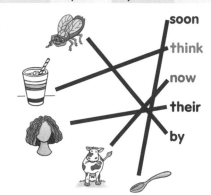

Page 95 — Solve It!

Page 96 — Broken Words

guess, thought, any, said, their, another

Page 97 — Snow Time

1st — Sue called Mary to come over and play.

2nd — They built a snowman.

3rd — They are drinking hot chocolate and eating cookies.

Page 98 — Look Closely

1. an, other, her, not 2. on
3. ear, we 4. than, an 5. aid
6. of 7. lease, ease, plea

Word Group 10

Answer Key

Page 99 — Building Blocks

    1. much 2. sing 3. none 4. piece 5. talk 6. either 7. walk 8. there

Page 100 — Flying High Word Search

Page 101 — Flying High

Page 102 — Rhyming Maze

Page 103 — Friends

    1. Eddie and Scott.

    2. Eddie's report will be on animals.

    3. Eddie chooses a book about sharks.

Page 104 — Keeping Cool

    these, never, much, enough, piece, paper

Page 106 — Missing Vowels

    1. new 2. sing 3. was 4. walk 5. paper 6. toward

Page 107 — Riddle Rhymes

    1. need 2. more 3. talk 4. walk 5. new

Page 108 — Fill-Ins

    1. enough 2. next 3. was 4. these 5. none 6. much

Word Group 10

Mixed Word Group
Answer Key

Page 109 — Rodeo Round-Up

water	father
house	night
animal	book
tooth	
picture	

Page 110 — Sail On!

either	soft
follow	thought
piece	who

Page 111 — Summer Fun

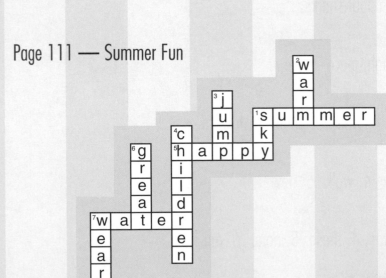

Page 112 — Happy Mother's Day

Today, some, special, They, yellow, does, much, read, about

Page 113 — Follow the Trail

Page 114 — Words Within Words

1. some, thing, so, me, thin, in
2. sat, day, at
3. or, ran, range, an
4. eat, at
5. here, her

Page 115 — Lost and Found

    night, again, build, write, other, enough

Page 116 — Hooray for Kate!

    1. story 2. about, water 3. picture 4. read 5. everyone

Page 117 — It's Magic!

    sum-mer, pa-per, pic-ture, fa-ther

Page 118 — Seasons

    grow, sky, snow, one, school, show

Page 119 — Paper or Plastic?

    Nouns — flower, picture, paper, night, mother

    Verbs — sleep, heard, buy, ask, jump

Page 120 — Picture/Word Match

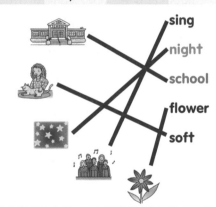

sing

night

school

flower

soft

Page 121 — ABC Challenge

    before, blue, boy, brother, busy, by

Page 122 — Same, but different

    flour—flower, hear—here, sum—some, won—one, peace—piece, cents—since

Page 123 — Fall Days

grow	try	around
know	by	found
snow	why	ground
blow	cry	

Mixed Word Group 151

Mixed Word Group

Answer Key

Page 124 — Artistic Crossword

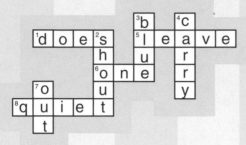

Page 125 — Word Find

Page 126 — At the Store

1. They are at the store.
2. They are going to buy peaches and apples.
3. They are going to make a pie.

Page 127 — Color by Words

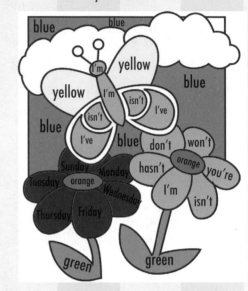

Page 128 — Can You Put These Words Back Together Again?

woman, really, hasn't, special, answer, through

Page 129 — Yellowstone

been, very, there, many, through, wear, walk, they, where, close, water, some, almost, every, two, these, much, more

More Fun With
Word Cards

Parents,

Have kids help to create 2 sets of their own word cards for each word group. Use a 3 x 5 index card for each word. Let your child decorate each one in any way they like – as long as the work is still legible.

These cards can be used by you and your child to play many games. Playing games is not only a great way to spend time with your child, it is also a good way to reinforce the spelling of the words they have been learning in this book.

You may use each set of word cards as you work through the groups in this book. You can also save them to use as a culmination and review after completing all of the exercises in the book.

On the following pages you will see some suggestions for games you and your child can play using the word cards. You may even come up with some ideas of your own! Have fun and enjoy being a part of your child's learning!

Word Cards 153

Word
Concentration

You will need both sets of cards from a word group.

Lay all of the cards face down on the table.
Have your child turn over two cards at a time.
If they show the same word, it's a match and
your child can keep the cards. If the cards do
not match, turn them back over and pick two
other cards. The object of the game is to
match each card to its partner.

Reading Flash Cards

You will only need to use one set of cards from a word group for this game.

Show a card to your child and have him or her say the word to you.

Variation: say a word and have your child spell it.

Word Sort

You will only need to use one set of cards from a word group for this game.

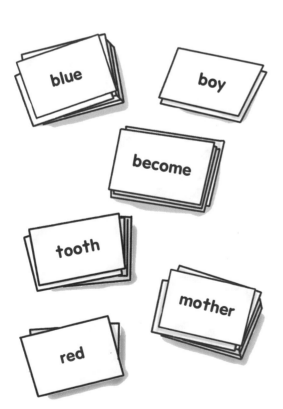

Put some word cards out on the table. Have your child sort the cards according to any number of attributes — parts of speech, colors, words that name people, numbers, plurals, two syllable words, etc.

Scrambled Letters

You will only need to use one set of cards from a word group for this game.

Choose a word and write the letters in random order for that word on a sheet of paper or white board, use magnetic letters, or type on a computer. Have your child unscramble the letters and read the word. Here are some suggested word scrambles:

after	Atfer
Monday	Mdnoay
tomorrow	Tmoorrow
cold	clod
summer	summer
before	berofe
don't	dno't
isn't	i'nst
warm	Wram
Saturday	Staurady
when	wehn
every	erevy
flower	flewor
winter	witner
Friday	Friady
hasn't	ha'nst
today	tadoy

Grab Bag

You will only need to use one set of cards from a word group for this game.

Have your child pick ten word cards out of a bag. They are then to write a story that includes those ten words.

Password

You will only need to use one set of cards from a word group for this game.

Have your child pick one word card from the pile. They read it and give clues to help you guess the word.

Variation: this can also be played by drawing pictures for appropriate words

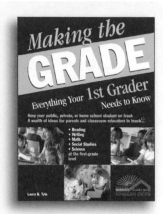
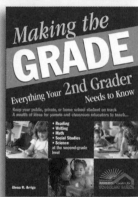

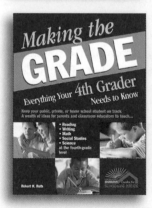
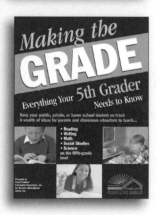
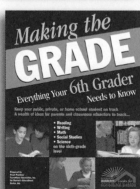

Minimum System Requirements for the Macromedia Flash Standalone
Player (Version 7)

WINDOWS
* 450 MHz Intel Pentium II processor (or equivalent)and later
* 128MB RAM
* Operating systems: Windows 98, Windows ME, Windows 2000, Windows XP

MACINTOSH
* 500 MHz PowerPC G3 and later
* 128MB RAM
* Operating systems: Mac OS X 10.2.x or higher

Launching Instructions for the PC

Windows Users:
Insert the CD-ROM into your CD-Rom drive.
The application should start in a few moments.
If this doesn't happen follow the steps below.
     1. Click on the start button on the Desktop and sellect Run.
     2. Type "D:\200Words" (where D is the letter of your CD-ROM drive)
     3. Click OK.

Launching Instructions for the MAC
Macintosh Users: The CD will open to the desktop automatically when inserted in the CD drive. Double click the 200 Words Flash icon to launch the program.